Speedy Cheetahs

by Michelle Levine

Lerner Publications Company • Minneapolis

Lerner Publications Company
A division of Lerner Publishing Group, Inc.
241 First Avenue North
Minneapolis, MN 55401 U.S.A.

Website address: www.lernerbooks.com

Words in *italic* type are explained in a glossary on page 30.

Library of Congress Cataloging-in-Publication Data

Levine, Michelle.
    Cheetahs / by Michelle Levine.
        p.   cm. — (Pull ahead books)
    ISBN-13: 978-0-8225-5933-7 (lib. bdg. : alk. paper)
    ISBN-10: 0-8225-5933-1 (lib. bdg. : alk. paper)
    1. Cheetah—Juvenile literature. I. Title. II. Series.
QL737.C23L47 2007
599.75'9—dc22   2005018008

Manufactured in the United States of America
3 — BP — 9/1/11

Zoom! A speedy cat races by.
What kind of cat is it?

This cat is
a cheetah.

A cheetah is a big cat.
Lions, tigers, and leopards
are other big cats.

Cheetahs have tan fur.
The fur is covered with
black spots.

Where do
these
spotted cats
live?

Most cheetahs live in Africa.
Many of them live in open,
grassy spaces.

These open spaces are called
savannas.

This cheetah is walking on a savanna. It is looking for *prey*.

The animals a cheetah hunts and eats are called prey.

Gazelles are prey for cheetahs.

Cheetahs also hunt antelopes, rabbits, and other animals.

A cheetah uses its ears to listen for prey.

Its ears twist and turn at each sound.

A cheetah uses its sharp eyes to look for prey.

This cheetah sees prey far away.
The cheetah hides in the tall grass.
It lies very still.

Then the cheetah begins to *stalk*. Slowly and quietly, it walks closer and closer to its prey.

ZOOM! Suddenly, the cheetah *sprints*. It runs very fast.

The cheetah is the fastest animal on land. It sprints as fast as a speeding car.

How does a cheetah move so fast?

A cheetah uses its long, strong legs to move fast. It uses its tail for balance.

A cheetah has long claws. When the cat runs, the claws dig into the ground.

The claws keep the cheetah from slipping.

This cheetah has caught its prey. It is carrying the prey to a hidden spot.

A cheetah eats quickly.
Other animals may soon come.
They might steal its food.

This mother cheetah has found another hidden spot.

It is a *lair*.
The lair is a place for her babies.

Baby cheetahs are called *cubs*.

The fuzzy cubs *nurse*.
They drink their mother's milk.

The mother *grooms* her cubs.

She licks their fur to keep it clean.

The cubs grow and grow.
They are ready to leave the lair
after about eight weeks.

The cubs stay by their mother.
She watches for danger. Lions and
hyenas hunt and eat cheetah cubs.

The cubs learn to sprint away from danger.

They play games. They grow strong.

These older cubs are hunting
with their mother.

They are learning to take care of
themselves.

Soon they will be big, speedy
cheetahs!

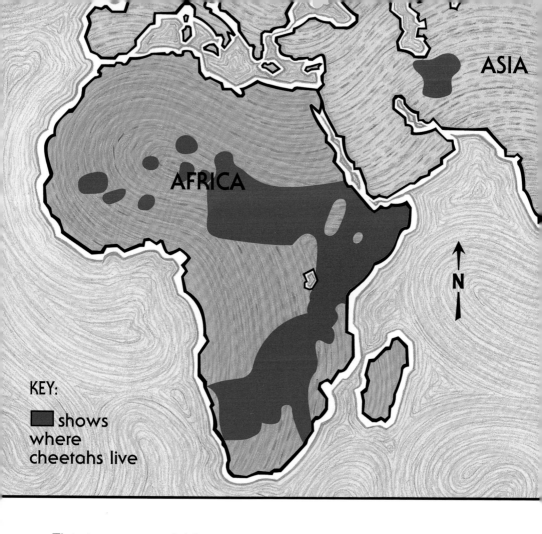

This is a map of Africa.
Where do cheetahs live?

Parts of a Cheetah's Body

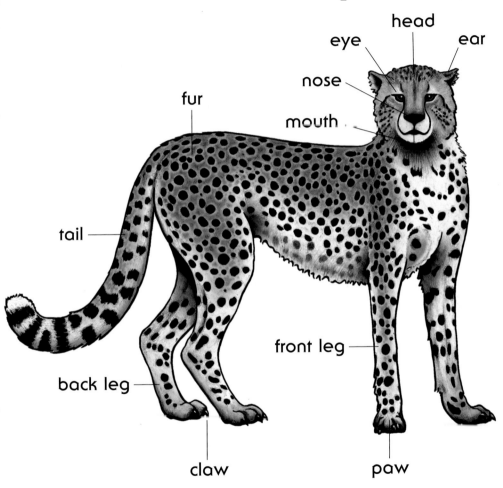

head

eye

ear

nose

fur

mouth

tail

front leg

back leg

claw

paw

Glossary

cubs: baby cheetahs

grooms: licks fur to keep it clean

lair: a safe, hidden place where mother cheetahs care for their babies

nurse: to drink mother's milk

prey: animals that are hunted and eaten by other animals

savannas: open grassland with some low bushes or trees

sprints: runs very fast for a short time

stalk: to walk in a quiet, secret way while hunting

Further Reading and Websites

Donaldson, Madeline. *Africa*. Minneapolis: Lerner Publications, 2005.

Smithonian National Zoological Park
http://nationalzoo.si.edu/Animals/AfricanSavanna/
meetcheetahs.cfm

Enchanted Learning
http://www.enchantedlearning.com/subjects/animals/
quiz/cheetah.shtml

Index

Photo Acknowledgments

The photographs in this book are reproduced through the courtesy of:
© Renee Lynn/CORBIS, front cover; © Photocyclops.com/SuperStock,
p. 3; © PhotoDisc Royalty Free by Getty Images, pp. 4, 5, 7, 9, 11, 12,
14, 23; © Royalty-Free/CORBIS, p. 6; © Breck P. Kent, p. 8; © Michele
Burgess, pp. 10, 13, 19, 24, 25, 26, 27, 31; © age fotostock/
SuperStock, pp. 15, 16; © Joe McDonald/Visuals Unlimited, p. 17;
© Tom Brakefield/SuperStock, p. 18; © Yann Arthus-Bertrand/CORBIS,
p. 20; © Gary Schultz, pp. 21, 22.